The Fighting Days

THE FIGHTING DAYS

a play by Wendy Lill

Talonbooks　●　Vancouver　●　1985

Published with the assistance of the Canada Council and the Manitoba Department of Culture, Heritage and Recreation.

Talonbooks
#104—3100 Production Way
Burnaby, B.C., Canada, V5A 4R4

Typeset in Baskerville and printed and bound in Canada by Hignell Printing Ltd.

Second Printing: September 1996

The author gratefully acknowledges the words and ideas of Francis Beynon. Passages from her columns in the *Grain Growers' Guide* and her novel *Aleta Day* have been used in the script.

Canadian Cataloguing in Publication Data

Lill, Wendy, 1950—
  The fighting days

  A play.
  ISBN 0-88922-226-6

  1. Beynon, Francis Marion — Drama. I.Title.
PS8573.I445F 1985   C812'.54   C85-091424-8
PR9199.3.L54F5 1985

The Fighting Days was first performed at the Prairie Theatre Exchange in Winnipeg, Manitoba on March 16, 1983, with the following cast:

Francis	Laurel Paetz
Lily	Terri Cherniack
Nellie	Linda Huffman
McNair	Morison Bock

Directed by Kim McCaw
Set and Costume Design by Katherine Christensen

CHARACTERS

FRANCIS BEYNON
LILY, *her sister*
NELLIE McCLUNG
GEORGE McNAIR, *editor of* The Rural Review

ACT ONE

Winnipeg, 1910-1914.

Scene One

Dark stage. Funeral music fading into the sound of a train. Lights up. FRANCIS, 18, and her sister LILY, 25, are on the train. FRANCIS is looking out the window, lost in thought. LILY is crocheting.

LILY:

Do you think Father's up there right now watching us?

FRANCIS:

I never really believed in that part. Did you?

LILY:

No, I guess not. Some things just sort of stick with you. He said he'd be joining Grandpa in heaven the day after he died, so there'd be no point in trying to put anything over on him.   *She smiles.*   I remember you saying that if he was going to heaven, you didn't want to go there. That you'd rather go to hell.

FRANCIS:

But I never really stood up to him. Had I been braver, Lily, I would have defied him.

7

LILY:

You were braver than the rest of us. It was you Father went after. You seemed to bring out the worst in him.

FRANCIS:

Why do you think that was?

LILY:

Mother says it was your questions that made him angry. He thought they sprang from an "undisciplined spirit"...whatever that means.

FRANCIS:

You know when he used to ask "are you right with God?" What did you say?

LILY:

I said "yes" every time and then he stopped bothering me.

FRANCIS:

But how does one know whether they're RIGHT with God?

LILY:

I don't know, Fanny.

FRANCIS:

Do you believe deep in your heart that Methodists are the only ones with immortal souls?

LILY:

Not any more. Not since I moved to the city.

FRANCIS:

What happened then?

LILY:

I guess I started to think...bigger. I met people who believed in all sorts of things. Some of my friends are Presbyterians. Vernon, the young man I'm seeing at the newspaper, is an agnostic.

8

FRANCIS:

> An agnostic? I've never even heard of that church.
> What does he believe?

LILY:

> Well...he believes...well, he's not sure there really is a
> God...he's just not sure.

FRANCIS: *concerned*

> Oh.

LILY:

> But he's very nice, Fanny. He went to school in
> England. He reads a lot, just like you.

FRANCIS:

> If you like him, Lily, I'm sure I will.

> *Silence.*

> Lily, what about the Catholics?

LILY:

> What about them?

FRANCIS:

> Are they all right too?

LILY:

> Yes, they're all right too.

FRANCIS:

> That's good. I always thought it was sad that Mrs.
> Sawatsky was going straight to hell after raising all
> those kids. Lily, what do you remember most about
> him?

LILY:

> "Serve the Lord with fear, with trembling kiss his feet,
> lest he be angry and you perish...for his wrath is
> quickly kindled." There was always so much wrath.

9

FRANCIS:

I'll always remember looking to see if his workboots were by the kitchen door. That meant he was in the house and I'd get that frightened feeling in my stomach. Lily, did you think he was ever going to die? I didn't. The horse died on its feet on the hottest day of the summer. Gippy and Rex crept off by themselves and died. I was scared that Mother would die in the yard with a load of wet laundry in her arms and that look on her face and I'd be left alone with him. I shouldn't have said that.

LILY:

You can't help the way you feel. *squeezing her sister's hand* Let's not talk about it any more.

Pause.

FRANCIS:

Lily, does this mean I'm free now?

LILY:

Free?

FRANCIS:

Free. Free to sing in the house, push peas around on my plate, screw up my face, play cards, read books...

LILY: *laughing*

All of those things! And Mother will be sixty miles away with Uncle George and not worrying over your soul any longer.

FRANCIS:

Thank heavens!

LILY:

I'm going to take care of you now. We'll get a nice bright room in the West End with elm trees out front. We'll go to picture shows and tea rooms and libraries...

FRANCIS:
Libraries!

LILY:
And you can meet my newspaper friends and join my
suffrage club.

FRANCIS:
Your what?

LILY:
My suffrage club. Oh, you'll learn about that soon
enough.

FRANCIS: *looking doubtful*
Do you think I'll fit in?

LILY:
Of course you will. You're going to love the city!

FRANCIS:
Do you think so?

LILY: *hugging her*
I do. And furthermore, the city will love you! Oh
Fanny, you're a brick!

Scene Two

*Women's Press Club. Sound of people climbing
stairs, voices, NELLIE AND LILY enter, mid-
conversation; FRANCIS follows behind.*

NELLIE: *reciting*
"I do not want to pull through life like a thread that
has no knot. I want to leave something behind when I
go. Some small legacy of truth, some *word* that will
shine in a dark place.." What word? What word? I
want that word to be....

They become aware there is no heat in the room.

LILY:
Warmth!

NELLIE: *going to radiator and banging it*
Didn't Isobel pay our rent this month?

LILY:
Maybe they think they can get rid of us by freezing us
to death.

*LILY and NELLIE continue working on speech.
FRANCIS walks around the room, fingering things.*

LILY:
I would start the other way, Nellie.

NELLIE:
With the alarm clock? You don't think McNair will call
me a drippy tap in need of a washer?

LILY:

Well, it would not be as bad as when he said you
rattled along like an old tin can.

NELLIE:

Or the time I squeaked along like a set of rusty
bagpipes.

LILY: *laughing*

But nothing will top the time he called Isobel as useless
as a button on a hat.

They all laugh.

NELLIE:

The perils of public speaking!

LILY:

You won't believe this fellow, Fanny.

FRANCIS:

Who is he?

NELLIE:

He's a wart on the nose of progress. He's a loose nut in
a machine trying to go forward!

LILY:

He's the editor of *The Rural Review*. We won't be much
longer, Fanny. Anyway, I'd leave the alarm clock in.
It's an idea that strikes people right between the eyes.

NELLIE:

You're right. I'll leave it in. *to FRANCIS* Your
sister gives me my best ideas, yet never gets any of the
credit!

LILY:

Nor any of the abuse. Suits me fine.

NELLIE:
Whenever I see you, Francis, I seem to be working on some silly speech. There's more to life than that. I haven't even had a chance to get to know you. *indicating sofa* I want you to sit down here and tell me all about yourself.

FRANCIS:
There's nothing to tell.

LILY:
Don't be shy, Fanny. *to NELLIE* She devours every book she can get her hands on. She knows more about newspapers than I do after four years at *The Free Press.* *to FRANCIS* You've got lots to tell!

FRANCIS:
Well, I grew up on a farm...

NELLIE:
So did I! We've already got something in common! When I was a girl, I loved to read books too, but I was always the first one yanked out of school to herd the cows. I would tear around from one field to another, chasing cows and hating every one of them!

FRANCIS:
I felt exactly the same way!

NELLIE:
Did you?

FRANCIS:
But they had to be moved or they'd eat through all the grass.

NELLIE:
Oh, I know they had to be moved, but I couldn't understand why I had to chase them all the time. It was always Nellie that had to do it. Never my brothers.

FRANCIS:

> But they had to go to school so they could handle the
> affairs of the farm.

LILY:

> But she wanted to go to school too! She wanted to learn ·
> to read.

NELLIE:

> I wanted to learn how to read more than I wanted to
> sing in heaven!

FRANCIS:

> But what was the point if you were just going to get
> married?

NELLIE:

> But if I was going to be a mother and a wife, wasn't I
> the most important of all? Didn't I have to be a light...
> a beacon?

LILY:

> With a husband and all those children in her care?

NELLIE:

> Just imagine, Fanny...imagine how wonderful it would
> have been if your mother had read Tennyson before
> you fell asleep at night...
>
> Willows whiten, aspens quiver,
> little breezes, dusk and shiver,
> through the wave that runs forever
> by the island in the river
> flowing down to Camelot.
>
> Four grey walls and four grey towers
> overlook a space of flowers
> and the silent isle imbowers
> the Lady of Shallot

FRANCIS: *entranced*

> That's beautiful! I always wanted to write...just like
> you and Lily! I thought if I could write things down,

they'd be clear to everyone...all the things I felt inside. I would be clear to everyone and I wouldn't feel so alone.

NELLIE:
Did you ever try?

FRANCIS:
Yes, but I didn't really have anything to say.

NELLIE:
Don't ever say that, Francis! Not ever. Any woman with a mind, a pair of eyes and a heart, already has more than it takes to write for any newspaper in this country!

LILY: *laughing*
Oh, Nellie!

NELLIE:
That's a good line! I should use it somewhere.

FRANCIS:
You make it sound so easy.

NELLIE:
It's not easy, but it's worth the effort. Isn't it, Lill?

LILY:
That depends on whether you ask me before or after my editor has torn apart my story.

NELLIE:
Details. But the point is we women have finally got a chance to write for one another now. Do you agree?

LILY:
I agree.

NELLIE:
Good!   *turning to FRANCIS*   Francis, we're not chasing cows any more. We've got no one to blame

but ourselves for not doing what we want. Do you undersand? *FRANCIS nods.* Which leads us back to the problem at hand, the speech for tomorrow night. You're coming, aren't you?

FRANCIS:
Oh, yes, I'll be there!

NELLIE:
Good!

Scene Three

The auditorium. FRANCIS and LILY enter and sit down. A gentleman in his late thirties sits down beside them and takes out a notebook. NELLIE takes the podium. Applause begins. FRANCIS is riveted.

NELLIE:

My name is Nellie McClung and I'm a disturber. Disturbers are never popular. Nobody likes an alarm clock in action, no matter how grateful they are later for its services! But I've decided that I'm going to keep on being a disturber. I'm not going to pull through life like a thread that has no knot. I want to leave something behind when I go; some small legacy of truth, some word that will shine in a dark place. And I want that word to be... DEMOCRACY! Democracy for Women. Because I'm a firm believer in Women, in their ability to see things and feel things and improve things. I believe that it is Women who set the standards for the world and it is up to us, the Women of Canada, to set the standards...HIGH!

Applause.

Maybe I'm sort of a dreamer, maybe I'm sort of naive... but I look at my little girls and boys and I think I want a different world for them than the one I was born into. I look at them and my heart cries out when I see them slowly turn towards the roles the world has carved for them: my girls, a life of cooking and sewing and servicing the needs of men; and the boys, scrapping and competing in the playground, then right up into the corridors of government, or even worse, the battlefields. I want them to have a choice about their lives. We mothers are going to fight for the rights of our little girls to think and dream and speak out. We're going to refuse to bear and rear sons to be shot at on faraway battlefields. Women need the vote to bring about a better, more equitable, peaceful society, and we're going to get it!

> *Standing ovation. LILY and FRANCIS applaud happily. The gentleman looks on without enthusiasm. NELLIE comes over.*

LILY:
> You were superb!

FRANCIS:
> Oh, yes!

NELLIE:
> Was I loud enough?

McNAIR: *aside*
> Excruciatingly.

> *NELLIE notices him; stiffens.*

NELLIE:
> Why, Mr. McNair. I thought I saw a bit of tartan in the crowd. I hope you found my speech enlightening.

McNAIR:
> It's always interesting to hear a woman speak in public. It's sort of like seeing a pony walking on its hind legs. Clever, even if not natural.

NELLIE:
> Well, I hope this time you'll manage to spell my name correctly. There are two "c"s. It is McCLUNG, not McLUNG.

> *McNAIR gets out his notebook and corrects the spelling.*

McNAIR:
> What a pity. I thought that was a rather good play on words.

19

LILY: *steering NELLIE away*
Let's go and find Isobel to see what she thought. Help
yourself to some lemonade, Fanny. I won't be long.

*NELLIE and LILY exit. FRANCIS goes over to a
refreshment table. McNAIR follows.*

McNAIR:
At least I can be assured of a little refreshment at these
events. Saves the evening from being a complete waste.

FRANCIS:
I thought her speech was wonderful.

McNAIR:
She rattles along like an old tin can. And she repeats
herself. She said the same thing at the Walker Theatre last
week.

FRANCIS:
It sounded spontaneous to me.

McNAIR:
That's a knack she's got.

FRANCIS:
Well, why did you come a second time if you thought so
little of it the first?

McNAIR:
I'm a reporter. I never give up hope.

FRANCIS:
A reporter?

McNAIR:
The name's McNair. George McNair.

FRANCIS:
The editor of *The Rural Review.*

McNAIR: *flattered*
That's correct. Does your husband take *The Review*?

FRANCIS:
I'm not married. But if I was, I'm sure he would, since it's the best farm paper this side of Kingston.

McNAIR:
What's in Kingston?

FRANCIS:
The Advocate, of course.

McNAIR:
The Advocate? It's a rag!

FRANCIS:
I disagree.

McNAIR:
It's a liberal propaganda sheet…and it's weak on markets.

FRANCIS:
You're weak on crop summaries.

McNAIR:
You don't say? May I be so bold as to ask your name?

FRANCIS:
Francis Beynon. Francis Marion Beynon.

McNAIR:
Ah, I see. You're the one who writes for *The Free Press*.

FRANCIS:
No, that's my sister Lillian. She was the one with Mrs. McClung. They're very close friends.

McNAIR:
Well, she's not a bad little writer.

21

FRANCIS:
> Oh, Lily's very good. But don't you think her paper's soft...soft on facts, soft on the truth, soft on banks, soft on the railways...

McNAIR:
> ...but hard on farmers.

FRANCIS:
> And even harder on suffragists.

McNAIR:
> Oh, you're one of those, are you?

FRANCIS:
> Yes, I guess I am.

McNAIR:
> Well, I'd better go and write this up.

FRANCIS:
> I'm curious, Mr. McNair. Why didn't you send your women's editor tonight?

McNAIR:
> Couldn't. She went and...passed away.

FRANCIS:
> Oh, I'm sorry to hear that.

McNAIR:
> Well, she was over seventy. She wouldn't have taken to this type of event much either. Anyway, she's history and I'm stuck without a living soul to attend these interminable meetings!

FRANCIS:
> Perhaps you might think of hiring someone with more modern ideas.

McNAIR:
> Easier said than done, little Miss.

FRANCIS:
Perhaps you might think of hiring me.

McNAIR:
You? Hiring you? I don't even know you.

FRANCIS:
Sir, I come from a farm and I am a woman. I know all about bedbugs and woodticks, runny eyes in chicks, cracked tits on milkers, cakes without eggs...and how to avoid the minister's visit.

McNAIR:
I'm sure you do.

FRANCIS:
My grammar's good. Lily taught me how to type. And I wouldn't wallow in sentimentality like that last one. No offence meant.

McNAIR:
Miss Beynon, you're making a speech. It's unwomanly.

FRANCIS:
It's not unwomanly, Mr. McNair. It's 1912. And I'm simply trying to interest you in my qualifications.

McNAIR: *interested*
Well, perhaps you should try to interest me in the cold light of day. Shall we say nine o'clock tomorrow morning? Mind you're not late!

FRANCIS:
No!

McNAIR walks towards the door, then turns.

McNAIR:
And don't forget to bring your lunch.

He exits.

FRANCIS: *to herself*
I think I've got myself a job!

Scene Four

*FRANCIS approaches the desk, sits down, and begins
to write her first editorial. She is tentative.*

FRANCIS:

To the Women of *The Rural Review*:
It is my great pleasue to begin my new task as editor of
the homemaker's page. I have lived on a western farm
myself and when I was a girl, rode the calves home
from the pasture and chased the wild geese off the
wheat fields back of the granary. In my mind's eye, I
can still see my mother, standing alone against the
faraway fields of wheat, sun hat in hand, her skirts
blowing away with the wind, looking for a rare visitor
to come down the road. I now know that she was only
one of the thousands of lonely women of the
prairies...far from neighbours, far from towns, far from
doctors.

Within this page, I hope you will all be able to get
closer to one another. I hope you will begin to see this
as YOUR page, where you can write and think and
dream and rage...and in every way, help one another.
The page is now YOURS.

Francis Marion Beynon

*Throughout the play, women of the prairies will
respond to FRANCIS' editorials through letters.*

WOMAN:

Dear Miss Beynon:
This is my first letter to your homemaker's
page—though I've had talks galore with you up
here... *pointing to head* I live on the prairie with
not many neighbours but I'm really not at all lonely. I
had a serious operation last May and then a few weeks

25

after, our little house and everything in it burned down. But in the midst of it all, God has blessed us with another little baby.   *weak smile*   Our eighth. So life is never dull. Could you please send me your little booklet How to Tell the Truth to Children? It is comforting to know that children can be told...the truth, and still retain the cleanness of thought and purity we wish for them. I've enclosed 5 cents for postage. My husband says what a rigamorole letter...though I can't write in a hurry...so please forgive.

Your sincerest reader, Sunbeam

Dear Miss Beynon:
I got something to say to your reader—Titewad's Wife. I have had three husbands and I think you got to have three husbands before you gets your fair av'rige. My first was terrible thin. My second was terrible fat. Men run that way. Always one thing or the other. Either terrible drinkers or don't drink at all. Either terrible tempers or no tempers at all. Some as cheap as pig dirt, others with an open hand. Don't see how us women folks stands 'em. Men's upsesses and downsesses has wore me out. My third husband was just plain av'rige. He just wasn't one thing or another. He was just so ordinary I couldn't stand him any longer and I divorced him. So to you lady I say, it's only after you have three husbands you know what you really want, and that's no husband at all.

Always Yours, Chucklehead

Scene Five

The Women's Press Club. FRANCIS is answering letters from her readers. LILY and NELLIE are helping. NELLIE is pregnant.

FRANCIS: *holding up letter*
How do you remove warts from animals and humans?

LILY:
Apply the water you pour off beans after they're boiled soft.

FRANCIS: *reading*
I am five months pregnant and I have a terrible time lacing my corset good and tight. Any suggestions?

LILY:
That's your department, Nell.

NELLIE:
Tell her to throw her corset in the closet. That's what I've done. *patting her stomach* Otherwise, our children will grow up with a terror of small rooms.

FRANCIS:
Is there any way to lengthen the life of my stockings?

LILY:
Tell her to rub paraffin on their soles.

FRANCIS:
What is the best colour of paint to go with oatmeal wallpaper?

NELLIE:
Either bone or brown.

FRANCIS:
>Do I have any advice on how to keep baby chicks in the pink?

NELLIE:
>For heaven's sakes, Francis, you don't have to answer everything. Give that one to the Hen Department at the paper!

FRANCIS: *laughing*
>There is no Hen Department. I don't know how I'd answer all of these without you.

NELLIE:
>Well, we wouldn't want you to lose your job.

LILY:
>Don't worry, Fanny, you'll be able to answer this kind of stuff in your sleep in no time.

NELLIE:
>I have better things to do. Let's stop now and practise.

FRANCIS:
>There's just one more. "Would someone be so kind as to tell me how I can clean feathers. I have an owl and would be very pleased if I could find out how to clean it?"

NELLIE:
>An owl? Is it a dead owl?

LILY:
>What would anyone want with a dead owl?

FRANCIS:
>"I have an owl" is all she wrote.

LILY:
>Maybe she wants to clean it out, then cook it.

NELLIE:

Cook an owl? How disgusting!

LILY:

No, I think it must be a stuffed owl if she's interested in its feathers. It's probably been sitting on her mantelpiece for years and the feathers are dirty.

NELLIE:

Cornstarch, then. How would you cook an owl anyway?

LILY:

Probably just like a duck.

NELLIE:

But there wouldn't be much to it, would there?

FRANCIS:

Maybe she has a pet owl...like some people have pet crows.

NELLIE:

Animals don't need anyone to clean them. They clean themselves. I wish people would be more precise.

LILY:

It must be dead, then. Tell her to rub the feathers in cornstarch and, if by chance, she wants to eat it, tell her to clean it out like a duck and cook it with lots of spices.

NELLIE:

Great! Let's get on with the practice.

NELLIE cranks up the Gramophone. FRANCIS puts away her papers. NELLIE hands out scarves, begins to demonstrate the dance.

LILY:

Don't strain yourself, Nell. You might shake it loose.

NELLIE:
Would that be so terrible?

FRANCIS and LILY:
Nellie!

NELLIE:
Well, I've had four already. How many does a modern woman need? My Jack is already 15. How about you and Vernon?

LILY:
I would like three but Vernon thinks it would interrupt his concentration.

NELLIE:
I think Vernon concentrates far too much! *They laugh.* And you, Francis?

FRANCIS:
No one will even want to marry me.

NELLIE:
Don't be silly! Come here and I'll show you how to do this.

> *FRANCIS gets up, moves about awkwardly at NELLIE's tutelage.*

This is an interpretive dance. You just let your body move in whatever way you feel. It's very naughty. I saw it at the Palladium last time we were in London. They go mad for dancing over there. If the British suffragists can do it, so can we. Imagine you're a swan.

FRANCIS:
I feel like a prairie chicken!

NELLIE:
Close your eyes. It helps you forget about yourself. Stick out your hips, Fanny. Farther.

FRANCIS:

    If McNair could see me now. He thinks it's queer for a woman to speak in public!

LILY:

    What's he going to think when he sees us doing an interpretive dance at the Press Club Christmas party?

        They laugh.

NELLIE:

    Maybe he'd go back to Glasgow where he belongs, working for some reactionary tabloid. He's like a Scotch thistle bristling for a fight. And you know, he drinks.

LILY:

    Don't be too hard on McNair. Fanny doesn't mind him. She told me that under all that bluster is a good heart.

NELLIE:

    Well his mind skids when it comes to suffrage! And he drinks.

LILY: *laughing*

    You've already said that! I think your mind skids when it comes to McNair.

FRANCIS:

    He's not that bad, Nellie.

NELLIE:

    What's good about him?

FRANCIS:

    Well...he wears plaid earmuffs to work on cold mornings. And sometimes during the day, I can hear him in his office humming to himself..."Bonnie Dundee."

NELLIE:

Francis, you've taken a shine to him. He's almost old enough to be your father!

FRANCIS:

No, I haven't.

NELLIE:

Then why are you blushing?

FRANCIS:

Because I feel preposterous doing this dance.

LILY: *coming to her rescue*

You're doing fine. Here, let me fix your scarf.

NELLIE:

I think she's going to miss you when you marry Vernon. Who will do up her buttons and make her hair nice?

LILY:

She can look after herself.

NELLIE:

Well, now that we've got warts and matching wallpaper out of the way, we'll have to get her working on the larger issues. Tomorrow you can come along to my Women for Peace Committee. We've started a world disarmament campaign, and then, after that, we'll drop in on the Christian Temperance meeting. We can always use new recruits, Francis. It's always the same old girls in everything.

FRANCIS:

I'd love to come.

NELLIE:

Good. All right now, let's all three try it together ... from the top.

Music crossover into next scene.

32

Scene Six

*The newspaper office. FRANCIS is practising her
dance step. The door opens; she hears McNAIR
approaching. She slides back behind her desk.
McNAIR enters.*

McNAIR:
>Let's see what you've got on your page this week.
>
>*He pulls the page out of the typewriter and begins to read
>aloud.* "We have too long been contented with the
>kind of motherhood that can turn its back on mere
>children toiling incredible hours in factories making
>bullets and ammunition and uniforms for some
>faraway war and yet calmly say, 'Thank God it's not
>my children.' What we need now is a new spirit of
>national motherhood." And someone who can write
>shorter sentences. National motherhood. National
>motherhood? You make it sound like the railway,
>Miss Beynon.

FRANCIS: *deflated*
>I quite liked that expression.

McNAIR:
>Is it yours?

FRANCIS:
>Well...

McNAIR:
>It sounds like something off of Mrs. McClung's bat.
>You seem to have an opinion about everything lately.
>National motherhood, intemperate husbands, the
>German war machine, the profession of parenthood,
>the Boy Scout movement, and suffrage ad nauseum.

33

But I find myself wondering...what happened to your columns on mothers and babies, ginger snaps and peonies? What about the little crocheted sweaters for the wee ones. Hmmmm? What about those things? They're important, too.

FRANCIS:

Do you think they are more important than freedom from cruel husbands and fathers, from hypocritical ministers, from war-mongering politicians?

McNAIR:

Oh, don't bludgeon me with adjectives. Just say what you mean.

FRANCIS:

I'm sorry.

McNAIR:

Unfortunately, the things you mention will always be with us. Scotch broth and shortbread and a garden full of bluebells make them a bit more tolerable. My mother knew that. She would never have bothered herself with voting and chasing men out of bars.

FRANCIS:

But was she happy?

McNAIR:

Happy? I don't know. She seemed content. She smiled a lot.

FRANCIS:

You mean she just put up with it.

McNAIR:

Perhaps. But the point is, she had enough to do in the home. You'll be wise to keep that in mind.

FRANCIS:

If you think that women belong in the home, why did you hire me?

McNAIR:

> I had no choice. What self-respecting man would want to write about "women's things"? Unfortunately, you don't seem interested in writing about them either.

FRANCIS:

> Mr. McNair, are you not finding my work satisfactory?

McNAIR:

> Did I say that?

FRANCIS:

> You imply that.

McNAIR:

> I do not. I think that the suffrage question is... interesting, but you take it much too far. Mrs. McClung need only pen one of her silly little verses and it somehow finds its way into your editorials.

FRANCIS:

> Mrs. McClung is at the forefront of the suffrage cause.

McNAIR:

> She is a dilettante and a debutante. And a hypocrite. She's an upper class snob who wouldn't have given my poor mother the time of day.

FRANCIS:

> That's not true. Nellie McClung is fighting for the vote for women.

McNAIR:

> For women who don't need the vote. For women who've got something better than the vote! Influence! And furthermore, the proper lineage!

FRANCIS:

> No!

McNAIR:

No? Then tell me why your suffrage club list is full of names like Steward, Titheradge, Ward, Galbraith, Gordon, and not...Lewycky, Schapansky and Swartz?

FRANCIS:

Well, maybe their husbands won't let them come.

McNAIR:

They're not there because your suffrage club doesn't want them there. Neither do they want them living next to them on Chestnut Street nor their children sitting beside theirs at school.

FRANCIS:

Mr. McNair, I believe in democracy for *all* women. I do!

McNAIR:

Then you're in the minority. Isobel Graham has gone on record saying she's afraid the entire western hemisphere is sinking under the weight of the immigrants.

FRANCIS:

Isobel has...a blind spot.

McNAIR:

And Laura McLaughlin, another one of your leading lights, is heading up the fight to eliminate any foreign language in the schoolyard.

FRANCIS:

That's because Laura thinks it's important that newcomers learn English.

McNAIR:

That's because she hates the very idea of them.

FRANCIS:

I admit there are some members who don't feel comfortable with all the strangers in our midst, but that

will change. It takes time to alter attitudes. It takes
time to remove the walls of class and privilege and
ethnic differences that...

McNAIR:

Oh, don't start that again! The fact is the suffragists
are an exclusive club. And you'd do well to stay away
from them.

FRANCIS:

I find it curious how you suddenly spring to the defence
of foreign women. Because in the year that I've known
you, you have never shown interest in *any* women
having the vote, whether their name was Gordon or
Schapansky! I'm beginning to think that you just enjoy
muddying the waters!

McNAIR: *winking*

I enjoy arguing with you. You argue like a man!

FRANCIS:

Well, I am not.

McNAIR:

And I'm glad you're not.

FRANCIS: *flustered*

I believe in the vote for women, all women, and I am
going to keep fighting for it.

McNAIR:

Now don't get so flustered. It's not that important, is
it?

FRANCIS:

Mr. McNair, let me try to explain something to you.
When I was a child, on the farm, I was constantly
asking questions. Does God ever change his mind?
Why was he angry all the time? Why couldn't I talk to
the Polish children on the next farm? Why didn't my
father help them out like the other neighbours? But
nobody wanted to answer my questions. There seemed

37

to be a secret fraternity at work that I didn't understand. My father and the Methodist minister and later my teachers thrashed and sermonized and ridiculed me until my spirit shrank and I began to doubt my very worth.

McNAIR:

It doesn't seem to have been a lasting affliction. You seem to have quite an unswerving confidence.

FRANCIS:

Well, I don't. I still cower at the voice of authority. Even now, I tense up as you, my editor, come into the room. Do you understand what I'm talking about?

McNAIR:

Yes, I think so, but I'm not sure what it has to do with suffrage.

FRANCIS:

Oh, but it's all connected! When I came to the city, I met women fighting for the freedom to think and worship and question for themselves. Women who challenge authority...who look it right in the eye and say, prove you're worthy of respect! I felt like I'd been let out of prison. I felt like a great gleam of sunlight had broken through the fog. And I didn't feel alone any more!

McNAIR:

You're a funny one. You remind me of those little birds I found trapped in the house when I was a child. My mother would make me catch them and let them go free outside. And whenever I caught them, I could feel their little hearts beating in my hand, and I wanted to tell them not to be afraid, that I wasn't going to hurt them. You're like one of those little birds. Miss Beynon, I understand you live alone since your sister married. Perhaps you might be needing someone to look in on you once in a while.

FRANCIS:

> I would like that very much.

McNAIR:

> Good, then. I will do that. It's time you associated with
> someone who still holds womanhood sacred.

FRANCIS:

> No! I don't need anyone to hold womanhood sacred. I
> hold womanhood sacred myself. I do!

McNAIR:

> Well, you hold it at quite a distance. It might help your
> cause if you applied some rouge to your cheeks
> occasionally. Good day, Miss Beynon, I'll let you get
> back to national motherhood.

> > *McNAIR exits. FRANCIS sits down at her desk and
> > begins typing angrily.*

FRANCIS:

> Men say that women have enough to do in their homes
> without worrying about going to the polling station. I
> have been doing some thinking about this. Prairie
> women have been trapped too long inside the home,
> lonely and dependent from the day they wed till the
> day they die. And yet, aren't we as necessary to prairie
> society as the sun and the rain are to the fields? Don't
> we deserve to be seen as whole people, with the same
> rights and responsibilities as the men we work beside?
> That's why I want the vote, because a vote is like being
> given a voice when before we were silent. It's like being
> set free after years of captivity. In the end, isn't what
> we're really talking about—freedom? I think so. But
> I've talked long enough. Please write and tell us what
> freedom means to you.
>
> > F.M.B.

WOMAN:

> Dear Miss Beynon:
> Some go to the Bible for proof that woman should not
> have the freedom to vote. I can see nothing there to

39

convince me that women have no interest outside her house. The very fact that God placed Eve outside in his big garden and not inside the four walls of a kitchen ought to prove she was intended to be a companion to her husband and to see and understand whatever interests him.

I have to thank you and your sister Lily and Nellie McClung for all the wonderful work you're doing in elevating women to their rightful place as queen of the home.

Sincerely, Western Sister.

P.S. Could any of the readers tell me how to take rust out of a white dress?

Dear Miss Beynon:
Freedom for me would be a public restroom in town. A place where a woman could go after a long trip in from the country. Please work on that.

Sunflower

Dear Miss Beynon:
I agree with you that freedom would come with getting the vote. If women had it sooner, there wouldn't be so many laws on the books which are a disgrace to civilization...not to mention humanity.

Dear Miss Beynon:
I am 31 years old, the mother of 7 children, the eldest 11 years, the youngest 8 months. I would like to have any information I can get about birth control. That would be freedom for me.

Dear Miss Beynon:
With all this talk of women's freedom, maybe there's something you're forgetting. And that's the foreigners. Haven't we got enough trouble with them over there, without letting them think they can run our country too? Can we bear dilution by the ignorance, low idealism and religious perversity of the average foreigner? I say no! We must keep them back. Give us

good sound British stock women, already civilized,
already subject to both earth and heaven for conduct.
Wolfwillow

FRANCIS:

I have to take exception to a recent view from
Wolfwillow about immigrants within our country. It
seems tragic to me the number of people, who without
being able to give a single reason, instinctively hate or
fear or distrust every person who does not belong to the
same race or religion as themselves. What is the harm
of people being different? Is anyone who is original in
their thinking really so frightening?

> *LILY is reading remainder of editorial at the*
> *beginning of the next scene.*

If our country of Canada is going to achieve its
potential as a great nation, we must begin to recognize
the contributions of people from all lands who decide to
make it their HOME.

For my part, I would say that the real foreigners are
not those who have been raised in different countries,
but those whose standards and ideals of life are so
immoveable as to not allow for communication with
others.

Scene Seven

*The Women's Press Club. LILY is reading
FRANCIS' editorial in the newspaper. NELLIE is
seated.*

LILY:

It's beautiful, Fanny.

FRANCIS:

You mean that?

LILY:

Yes I do! I knew you'd put your heart and mind to
work and come out with something that rang absolutely
true!   *hugging her*   She's quite a girl, isn't she,
Nell?

NELLIE:

At least she doesn't come to us for advice on hens any
more.

LILY:

Is that all you've got to say?

FRANCIS:

Do you like it, Nell?

NELLIE:

I'm surprised that McNair let you run such an
idealistic little piece.

FRANCIS:

He said he thought it was sort of...hopeful.

LILY:

Well it is hopeful, and I'm proud of you! Nell, aren't you?

NELLIE:

She's a quick learner.

FRANCIS:

Nellie, do you like it?

NELLIE:

Like it? I think the sentiments are admirable, but I wonder if it takes everything into account.

FRANCIS:

What do you mean?

NELLIE:

Such as what's going on in Europe right now. Some of the countries where these foreigners hail from are rattling their sabres at Britain even as we speak. People are frightened. God only knows what might happen over there. That's all, Fanny.

LILY:

Well, I think we should go have an ice cream to celebrate her efforts.

NELLIE:

You two go along. I've got some work to finish first.

LILY and FRANCIS leave. FRANCIS is crestfallen.

Scene Eight

FRANCIS' suite. FRANCIS is straightening things and looking in the mirror. She is nervous. The doorbell rings; it's McNAIR.

FRANCIS:
Good afternoon, Mr. McNair.

McNAIR:
Good afternoon, Miss Beynon. I hope I'm not disturbing you.

FRANCIS:
No, not at all. Won't you come in.

McNAIR:
I guess you're wondering why I dropped a note about visiting today.

FRANCIS:
I thought perhaps you were going to be in the neighbourhood.

McNAIR takes a letter from his pocket and hands it to her.

McNAIR:
Not exactly. Here's a letter I received from a group of your readers from Minnedosa. It seems they take exception to your column on the foreign question.

FRANCIS reads, looks upset.

FRANCIS:
I thought it was the most heartfelt thing I'd written.

McNAIR:

It was mercifully short of adjectives.

FRANCIS:

It sounds as if they hate me.

McNAIR:

Not you, Miss Beynon, just what you're saying.

FRANCIS:

Maybe I was a bit outspoken. Even Nellie seemed cool when she read it.

McNAIR:

Did you believe in what you wrote?

FRANCIS:

Yes.

McNAIR:

Well then?

FRANCIS: *reading on*

They're asking for my resignation. That's why you've come, isn't it?

McNAIR:

I wouldn't be much of an editor if I could be intimidated by bigots such as these. I follow a hardy little gleam myself called freedom of the press. You're doing a good job, Miss Beynon. I'm not saying I agree with everything you write. Believe me, I don't. I'm not a big reformer, as you know. But as long as you write with fairness and reason, and punctuation...I'll back you. I came to tell you that.

FRANCIS: *indicating the letter*

But what about this?

McNAIR:

> Forget about the letter. Your column obviously struck a chord in some of your readers, and they didn't like the sound of it. But that's not your problem.

FRANCIS:

> Except that I have this tight feeling in my stomach that I haven't felt since I was a child.

McNAIR:

> If you want to be liked by everyone, you're in the wrong line of work.

FRANCIS:

> Perhaps I am.

McNAIR:

> Don't say that. You'll grow a thicker skin in time. Look at me.

FRANCIS:

> Is that what that is?

McNAIR:

> I think you're a fighter, and when the occasion arises, you'll come out strong.

FRANCIS:

> Thank you. I hope you're right. Could you stay for a while and have some tea?

McNAIR:

> That would be lovely, Miss Beynon.

FRANCIS:

> Please call me Francis.

McNAIR:

> All right, Francis, please call me McNair.

> *FRANCIS exits to kitchen.*

How does one occupy one's time when not fighting for
women's rights?

FRANCIS:

> I've been known to go to concerts in the park and even
> some plays. Lily and I have been to every tea room in
> the city. Sometimes her husband Vernon takes us out
> to the country in his roadster.

McNAIR:

> Perhaps some afternoon you might enjoy a trip up to
> Winnipeg Beach. I hear it's a popular spot with the
> fashionable crowd. Though being seen with me would
> perhaps not be quite so fashionable.

FRANCIS *re-entering with tea tray*
> I would be delighted to be seen with you.

McNAIR:

> Perhaps some time the two of us could go to church...
> or did the fierce God of the Methodists scare you off
> altogether?

FRANCIS:

> No, I've made my own truce with God. In fact, I met
> God one afternoon in a corner of the pasture.

McNAIR:

> Did you?

FRANCIS:

> I'd gone out before a thunderstorm to find the cows. I
> remember looking all around and seeing nothing but a
> few shacks between me and the faraway edges of the
> world. Then over the east, a snake of fire wiggled down
> the sky, followed by a crash of thunder. Then a breeze
> stirred my hair and I felt I was riding on the wings of a
> bird. I knew God passed by in that breeze because for a
> moment, I wasn't afraid of anything—not my father, or
> the minister, or doing compositions, or Lily's warts.. or
> anything at all.

McNAIR:

> I don't know whether you're a heathen or not, but you breathe a clean wholesome look upon life. My mother would have liked you, Francis. Perhaps getting that letter wasn't so unpleasant after all. It's given us a chance to....

> > *McNAIR notices an orange sash on a chair, with the words VOTES FOR WOMEN. He goes over and picks it up.*

McNAIR:

> What trumpery is this?

FRANCIS:

> That's my sash for the suffrage parade.

McNAIR:

> Your sash?

FRANCIS:

> Yes. We're all wearing them...for effect.

McNAIR:

> Surely, Francis, you're not going to make a spectacle of yourself like that?

FRANCIS:

> Well, that all depends on what one calls a spectacle.

McNAIR:

> I call an army of matrons marching down Main Street in orange sashes a spectacle. My God, you'll have the whole city staring gape-mouthed at you. Laughing and hooting and hollering. It's outrageous.

FRANCIS:

> Now wait a minute!

McNAIR:

> A whole generation of women being turned upside down, turned into shrill opinionated harpies, when

they should be at home, having lots of good strong children!

FRANCIS:

Like a bunch of good breeding hogs!

McNAIR:

There's nothing wrong with good breeding. And there's not enough of it happening any more. Instead, we're being swamped by a bunch of immigrants who don't even know "God Save the King." None of you ladies seem to care that we'll be at war in a month, and there'll be real armies marching down Main Street.

FRANCIS:

Of course we care, but we can't just drop women's suffrage because a bunch of countries can't settle their differences.

McNAIR:

You're a babe in the woods.

FRANCIS:

And you're a...you're unspeakable! You're everything that people say about you.

McNAIR:

Well if what you mean is that I don't delude myself and that I'm not a dreamer, I suppose you're right.

FRANCIS:

Well, I am a dreamer! And I believe there are changes coming. Wonderful changes...that will allow everyone to live in freedom. Those days are coming but we have to fight for them.

McNAIR:

There is something very wrong with you. I would not permit my wife, if I had one, to carry on the way you do

FRANCIS:

Well I would certainly not permit my husband, if I had one, to substitute his conscience for mine! Good day, McNair!

With a melodramatic sweep of her hand, she indicates the door. McNAIR leaves. FRANCIS picks up the sash, turns it over in her hands, looks miserable.

Scene Nine

At the suffrage parade. FRANCIS is standing in the
crowd, listening to NELLIE speak. The atmosphere is
jolly, excited.

NELLIE: *with megaphone*
All right, sisters, you've got your instructions for the
parade. Afterwards, we're invited to Government
House for tea and sandwiches with the Premier and the
Mayor of Winnipeg. You look beautiful out there.
We've come a long way, sisters. The day has finally
arrived when we've beaten back the bigotry which says
that men are better than women. This day strikes a
blow for social equality!

> *The suffrage march begins. It is a victorious moment.*
> *FRANCIS is in the midst of it, elated.*

FRANCIS:
Oh I am thankful to be living in these fighting days,
when there are so many things waiting to be done, that
we have no time to sit and feel sorry for ourselves,
when Humanity is seething and boiling and stirring
with a thousand conflicting interests, which in the end
will work themselves out to the final good of the race.
And we women have just begun to dabble with our
fingertips in this great eddying stream of life!

> *Suddenly the suffrage music turns into military music.*
> *Parade sounds become the sound of heavy boots. The*
> *expression on FRANCIS' face changes from victory to*
> *confusion and fear. A drill sergeant calls out*
> *"Company, halt!"*

ACT TWO

Scene One

*FRANCIS is in her apartment. It is Christmas time.
She is writing her Christmas editorial, 1916.*

FRANCIS:

> The Christmas edition of *The Review* will have to go out
> this year without a Christmas editorial on the women's
> page. Vainly I have tried to call up the old jubilant
> spirit of Christmas...without success. To observe this
> great celebration, while Christian Europe is busy
> contradicting its teaching "Peace on Earth, Good Will
> to Men," seems almost a sacrilege. The pen writes
> haltingly and unconvincingly upon the subject...and
> finally stumbles and stops altogether.

> *Light up on LILY, seated on the sofa, rolling
> bandages. FRANCIS is pacing.*

LILY:

> We took bones last night. It's astonishing how many
> ways there are of being injured. We learned that
> anything ending in "itis" is an inflammation. First aid
> is a rude sort of thing. You just grab an old gent's cane
> or umbrella for splints and a lady's clothing for

53

bandages. Carrie Markham says she just knows she'll be wearing her best and Frenchest lingerie when she'll have to tear it into bandages for some poor private.

Then we did drowning...with a REAL man to demonstrate. In one method, you have to hold the tongue of the drownee out with a handkerchief. The tongue is a rather slippery member. Sometimes one has to put a needle through it to keep it outside the mouth. That's in case there is a lot of blood in the throat....

FRANCIS:

Lily, what are you talking about?

LILY:

My first aid class.

FRANCIS:

The war is three thousand miles away. Why are you taking first aid?

LILY:

It's good to be prepared.

FRANCIS:

Prepared for what?

LILY:

Prepared in case we have to do our bit.

FRANCIS:

Are you off to France to save men...drowning on the battlefield?

LILY:

Of course not.

FRANCIS:

Is the conflict going to spread to Canada?

LILY:

That's not the point.

FRANCIS:

> Then what is the point of these endless first aid classes? To me, it all seems...daft.

LILY:

> Everything seems daft to you lately. Even what I'm doing!

FRANCIS:

> That's 'cause you're doing the strangest things.

> *LILY gets up to leave.*

> Where are you going?

LILY:

> I shouldn't have come. I hoped maybe we could talk about...just talk...but you're being...oh, I don't know how to describe it!

FRANCIS:

> I'm sorry, Lily. Please don't go. I need to talk, too.

LILY:

> All right then. You start.

FRANCIS:

> Lily, do you remember when Ned Stone's father came back from the Boer War? He said he'd seen British soldiers rounding up women and children and putting them in compounds. He said he saw them dying like flies. I walked home across the field, trying to imagine people dying like flies...you and Mother and Mrs. Gregory and the Hawkin girls....Lily, that's what's happening over there! Last month, one hundred thousand men died in one day!

LILY:

> I know. I read the paper.

FRANCIS:

> Lily, what do you really think of the war?

LILY:

I don't want to think about it.

FRANCIS:

Why not?

LILY:

It gives me a headache.

FRANCIS: *exasperated*

Well, that's a small price to pay compared to some!

LILY:

There you go again!

FRANCIS:

I'm sorry. It's just that I look at those boys on the parade ground. They're almost too young to shave yet, but there they are, marching around, waving their bayonets, making funny noises, jumping to attention. It all seems so...pointless.

LILY:

How can you say that? They're fighting for democracy, so that you and I can live in freedom. Isn't that what they're fighting for?

FRANCIS:

So they say. I heard Vernon talk last night at the Labour Temple. I thought you'd be there.

LILY:

I couldn't miss my class.

FRANCIS:

Couldn't pass up splints and tourniquets to hear your husband speak out against the war?

LILY:

I know what he said. He gave me a private rendition last night when he came home. The British peers own part of the armaments plants in Germany. The first

56

guns captured from the Germans were made in England. The only people who will win the war will be the munitions makers. Conscription is a violent attack on the rights of the individual....

FRANCIS:

Well?

LILY:

Well...it makes sense...and I believe him. But I just don't know how to put it all together...what Vernon's saying, what others are saying. I...it would be a lot easier if he wasn't giving public lectures.

FRANCIS:

Lily! Vernon has a right to speak in public.

LILY:

Except that half the paper won't talk to him now and the copy editor checks my stories twice before they go to press. He assumes I think like Vernon.

FRANCIS:

Well, don't you?

LILY:

Well, yes, but...

FRANCIS:

Then you've got to stand up for him, Lily! You've always fought for people's right to express themselves. The issue here is freedom!

LILY:

But I thought it was freedom that we're fighting for over there? Well, whatever it is, there are millions of young men going out and fighting for it. How can they all be wrong?

FRANCIS:

But how can you ever be free by killing people or being afraid that someone's going to kill you?

LILY:

I can see why Father hated your questions.

FRANCIS:

Now's not the time to be quiet, Lily. My God, even McNair's not hoodwinked by all this flagwaving hysteria! He's getting his teeth into war graft and profiteering.

LILY:

Well that's fine for him. He's too old to have to worry about it.

FRANCIS:

What do you mean?

LILY:

Conscription is coming, Fanny.

FRANCIS:

Lily, is that what you're worried about? Vernon wouldn't go, would he?

LILY:

No. He's a pacifist.

FRANCIS:

Well, that's good, isn't it?

LILY:

I suppose.

FRANCIS:

You don't sound happy!

LILY:

I am. I am. It's just that if he won't go, does that make him...a coward?

FRANCIS:

Do you think he's a coward?

LILY:

No. But I think...if Vernon won't go, what about Nellie's Jack? He enlisted the day he turned eighteen.

FRANCIS:

Oh, I hate this!

LILY:

So do I! *She bursts into tears* Isn't it strange, Fanny. One day we're collecting signatures for the vote, and the next, we're signing people up for the patriotic fund. I can't even remember any more who signed what. Last July at Nellie's cottage, Vernon was playing ball with Jack on the beach, and all of us were lolling in the hammocks....I don't know what to think any more, Fanny. I'm trying not to think. That's why I'm taking these silly classes from women in red, white and blue dresses. I have to DO something!

FRANCIS: *going over to comfort LILY*
I know, Lily.

The doorbell rings.

That must be McNair. He's early. I'll be right back.

McNAIR enters, sees LILY.

McNAIR:

Lily! *noticing she is crying* I hope I'm not interrupting something. I could go away and come back later.

LILY:

No, please don't leave on my account. I'm all right now.

McNAIR:

I just thought I'd peruse the papers in pleasant company before we went to the party. *He sits down on the sofa and opens the papers.* Just pretend I'm not here.

Awkward pause.

Here, this will cheer you up!   *reading*   "The Boer
War has brought us the khaki brown and the mopish
scout hats, and just as we were feeling at home in these
sombre shades, war was declared in the Balkans, and
that brought us, blessedly, I might add, those pretty
peasant waists and rich, bright-hued embroideries of
the southern climes. Let's hope we never to go war
with the Eskimos." Fantastic mind behind that report.

FRANCIS:
Why would that cheer us up?

McNAIR:
Well, at least neither of you is responsible for it.

FRANCIS laughs.

Listen to this.   *reading*   "The patriotism of those
war manufacturers who are skinning kin and country
with their faulty gear and second-rate boots is the kind
that should be recognized by a coat of tar and feathers.
But instead, they'll probably get a title!" My God, that
man can write!

FRANCIS:
Who wrote it?

McNAIR:
I did!

*LILY and FRANCIS both laugh. LILY collects her
things.*

LILY:
Oh, you're a ray of sunshine on a cloudy day, McNair.
I'm going home to get ready now.

McNAIR: *standing*
We'll see you later then.

FRANCIS goes to the door with her. They hug.

FRANCIS:
> We'll see you soon.

> *FRANCIS comes back into the room and starts
> pacing. McNAIR watches.*

McNAIR:
> You've got a bee in your bonnet.

FRANCIS:
> Would you ever think of fighting in the war?

McNAIR:
> It's a bit late in the day for me to enlist.

FRANCIS:
> But if you weren't too old, would you even consider it?

McNAIR:
> I suppose I would.

FRANCIS:
> Why?

McNAIR:
> Why? Because it's getting bloody hard to stay out of it!
> If you're of age and not in uniform, women look at you
> as if you're not quite complete. And the men simply
> hate you.

FRANCIS:
> But why is that? What business is it of theirs? It's your
> life!

McNAIR:
> Am I coming in on the tail end of an argument?

FRANCIS:
> Yes, you are. I'm sorry.

She sits down beside him.

McNAIR:

> If I was younger, I would go to war, Francis. I have a
> responsibility to fight for the freedom of my country.

FRANCIS:

> What does that really mean?

McNAIR:

> Well, it means to protect our homes, our loved ones...
> our women. Men are supposed to sacrifice their lives
> for women. Haven't you noticed? Since the war
> started, I haven't heard a peep from your Women for
> Peace Committee. Why do you think that is?

FRANCIS:

> They're knitting socks and rolling bandages.

McNAIR:

> But why do you think that is?

FRANCIS:

> I don't know. I don't know.

McNAIR:

> Because when it comes right down to it, women need
> protection, and they know it. At least most of them do.
> And that's why they swoon into the arms of the first
> waiting soldier.

FRANCIS:

> Why do you say things like that to me?

McNAIR:

> I can't resist. Your cheeks colour up in such a pretty
> way.

FRANCIS:

> Well, I'm tired of knitting socks. It's time to DO
> something!

McNAIR:

> All right. Put on your coat and we'll go to the party.

FRANCIS:

> I'm serious.

McNAIR:

> You've taken some pot shots at the Patriotic Fund.
> You're always haranguing us about the treatment of
> foreigners. *FRANCIS dismisses this.* My
> editorials started the ball rolling towards the
> investigation on rotten boots. I think we're doing our
> bit by keeping the war honest.

FRANCIS:

> McNair, I remember my first column about the war.
> *recollecting* "We women will keep our purpose clear
> —true democracy—and with our purpose, transport
> our men, our country, through the troubled waters of
> war!" I saw womanhood as some great unsinkable ship
> which would buoy up everyone!

McNAIR:

> That's an admirable image.

FRANCIS:

> Except that it was wrong! We thought we were sailing
> the vessel of freedom, but there seems to be a thousand
> others out there with the same claim. How can freedom
> take so many forms? I don't know what to think any
> more. Lily's on the verge of tears all the time and
> Nellie's a flagwaving patriot. We've got the vote now,
> but we're too anxious or terrified to figure out what to
> do with it. The letters I get are filled with war and loss
> and fear...

McNAIR:

> And while you're at it, you're the worst of all! You're
> constantly brooding over every war report as if you'll
> learn something new by counting up the stacks of dead.

FRANCIS:

You're right. I am the worst of all. I feel so utterly
useless!

*McNAIR puts his arm around her, leads her to the
sofa.*

McNAIR:

Come here and sit with me. You can't do anything
more than you're already doing. War is always hard on
high-strung women.

FRANCIS:

That's a fine remark.

McNAIR:

It was meant by way of comfort. I know it's hard on
you.

FRANCIS:

And not on you. In your heart, you believe this war is
right, don't you?

McNAIR:

Of course it's not right. War is never right. But God
almighty, woman, it's Christmas Eve. Can't you just
be content to watch the candles flicker and the
snowflakes fall? Do you have to notice every tragic face,
every heinous act? Why can't you just notice...me!

FRANCIS:

I'm sorry, McNair. I do notice you. All the time. I do!

McNAIR:

Well then, why don't you try to imagine a little house
with a garden full of bluebells, and a trellis and a little
baby in your arms...a little pal. That's what I do.
Makes me feel better.

FRANCIS:

You're such a romantic.

McNAIR:
> And what's wrong with that?

FRANCIS:
> Nothing, except why do you always picture me in a garden with a baby? Do you think I'd be happy just doing that? If I stopped thinking altogether?

McNAIR:
> Well, give it a try. Just put your wee mind to it...little pink and white gurgling bundles...tiny fingers...

FRANCIS: *laughing*
> Oh, how unfair that men can't give birth! You'd be such a perfect mother.

McNAIR:
> Oh, the world is too unfair.

> *They kiss.*

Scene Two

The Press Club Christmas party.

LILY:

And now for a bit of light entertainment from the carefree sisters of the typewriter and the interrogation mark. Nellie McClung, with our assistance, will give her musical rendition of her much loved poem...
LET'S PRETEND.

NELLIE: *accompanied by LILY and FRANCIS*
Let's pretend the skies are blue,
Let's pretend the world is new,
And the birds of hope are singing all the day.
(CHORUS) All the day!
Short of gladness, learn to fake it,
Long on sadness, go and shake it!
Life is what you make it, anyway.
Let's pretend the skies are blue,
Let's pretend the world is new,
There is wisdom without end...in the game of
    Let's Pretend!

McNAIR applauds. The three women join him.

LILY:
That was splendid, Nellie!

FRANCIS:
Oh, yes!   *to McNAIR*   Wasn't it?

McNAIR:
A frothy little delight, I must say.

NELLIE:
A rare compliment!

McNAIR:

As rare as your rhymes!

FRANCIS:

Shall I pour the lemonade?

NELLIE:

Thank you, dear.

LILY:

There will be no bickering tonight...and no talk of the war. Is that clear? This is a Christmas party.

McNAIR:

I'll drink to that.

NELLIE:

You would.

McNAIR:

And where is your better half tonight, Nell?

NELLIE:

At a patriotic drive.

McNAIR:

And yours, Lill?

LILY: *reticent*

At an anti-conscription rally.

McNAIR:

Well, thank God some of us are doing something irresponsible tonight.

Awkward silence.

I heard a funny story the other day. In the spring, they're going to build a roof garden on the legislative building. To supply fresh cut flowers for the politicians.

FRANCIS:
  The cabinet ministers can go up and take some air on
  their roof farm!

LILY:

  It will be quite inspiring to see Premier Norris in
  overalls doing his agricultural duty.

  They laugh. Another awkward silence.

FRANCIS:
  There's a new play at the Walker I want to see.

LILY:
  What's it called?

FRANCIS:
  It's called *The Guns of*...oh, we'll talk about it another
  time.

  Another awkward silence.

LILY:
  I hear Sadie Vaugh is expecting!

FRANCIS:
  That didn't take long.

NELLIE:
  I think that's called war-risk insurance.

McNAIR:
  More lemonade, Nell?

NELLIE:
  Please.

McNAIR:
  I don't hear much about suffrage now that you've got
  the vote. I guess you can't blame every social ill in
  Manitoba any longer on your political disability.

NELLIE:
Well, we still haven't got the federal vote. But it's coming.

McNAIR:
Yes, so I hear. But when it does, you'll find the privilege as empty as last year's bird's nest.

NELLIE:
We'll see.

McNAIR:
You'll end up choosing between two scoundrels, one not much better than the other. I've often felt, when I vote, that I'm not exercising much more political influence than the horses that haul me to the polling station.

NELLIE:
Nor probably much more intelligence.

McNAIR:
You're being rude, Nell.

NELLIE:
And you're being patronizing.

FRANCIS:
You're both being...

LILY: *to FRANCIS*
Themselves!

McNAIR:
I'm simply telling your friend not to feel badly that she hasn't turned the world around.

NELLIE:
We closed the bars.

McNAIR:
Aye, that you did. Deprived many a young lad one last good belt before going off to the slaughter.

NELLIE: *angrily*
Don't talk like that about our boys!

LILY:
Please don't fight, you two.

McNAIR:
It would have done them no harm...the odd nip! You should try it yourself sometime!

FRANCIS:
The music is starting up. Why don't we dance?

NELLIE:
You're disgusting!

McNAIR:
And you are a hypocrite!

NELLIE:
I am not!

McNAIR:
Aren't you? Then tell us why you told the Prime Minister to exclude foreign women from the upcoming federal election. So much for women's suffrage!

FRANCIS:
That's not true!

McNAIR:
I read it in the *Free Press*.

LILY:
Nell, you didn't tell me.

NELLIE:

There wasn't time. He was only in town for a couple of hours.

LILY:

But you could have called....

NELLIE:

Well, I didn't. And it's done. McNair likes to sensationalize. I simply suggested that the foreign women be excluded as a temporary war measure. A war measure. It's not a new idea. Let's not ruin our evening.

LILY:

McNair, will you dance with me? I need some time to clear my head.

McNAIR and LILY exit. FRANCIS and NELLIE are left in stunned silence.

FRANCIS:

There was a speech you made once about leaving a word behind to shine in a dark place. It was years ago. Do you remember?

NELLIE:

There've been so many, they kind of float together.

FRANCIS:

It was at the William Avenue Library. It was a summer night. Lily and I walked there from our suite on Arlington. I smelled lilacs; the man next door was out watering his lawn...his wife was sitting on the verandah, watching, rocking....You said that night...I want to leave some word behind to shine in a dark place...and I want that word to be democracy.

NELLIE:

You have a good memory.

FRANCIS:
I was so moved by that statement, I would have
jumped off a cliff that night, if you'd asked me.

NELLIE:
You've been a hard worker.

FRANCIS:
I don't understand anything any more, Nellie. Help
me!

NELLIE:
Oh, Francis, there was a reason for this. I suggested
excluding the foreign women only until the war is over.

FRANCIS:
But what does the war have to do with it?

NELLIE:
Francis, there are districts where almost every single
English-speaking man has enlisted. The moral tone of
the electorate has drastically changed.

FRANCIS:
Moral tone?

NELLIE:
The only way to protect our...traditions...is to limit the
vote to Empire women.

FRANCIS:
But don't the foreign women have the same
"traditions"? Justice, love, equality? How can you
turn your backs on them...if you truly believe in
women?

NELLIE: *with difficulty*
It's not that simple. The foreign community...does not
view conscription favourably.

FRANCIS:

Oh, I see! How efficient you are! If one doesn't view conscription favourably, then lop off their vote or their heads, whichever is easiest!

NELLIE:

You make me tired, Francis. You were a raw green girl from the country when I first met you, too scared to open your mouth without your sister's prompting. It was Lily and I who brought you out, who filled you with every ideal you have today. And you dare to stand there and question me on what's right and wrong!

FRANCIS:

But this is wrong! What you're doing is a total contradiction!

NELLIE:

Oh, don't tell me about contradictions. You have no right. You have nothing to lose in this war. You know nothing of the pain and nausea I feel when I read the casualty lists. You moon around over that drunken tory who'd rather have a woman strapped to the sink than marching in a suffrage parade. You have no right! It is I who is paying every minute this war continues. We have to end it, don't you understand! We have to win this wretched horrid war!

> *FRANCIS is stunned into silence; NELLIE is shaking. The music stops. McNAIR and LILY return.*

FRANCIS:

What about Women for Peace, Nell?

NELLIE:

Stop it.

FRANCIS:

Was that just another phrase that flowed off your tongue?

LILY:

Fanny, don't talk like this! Please!

FRANCIS:

Did you ever really believe we could stop war or change anything at all?

NELLIE:

Of course I did! I do!

LILY:

Stop this!

McNAIR:

Francis, calm down!

FRANCIS:

Why are you all trying to shut me up!

McNAIR:

There's nothing anyone can do about the war now! Germany declared war on Britain. We couldn't have stayed out of it. We have a responsiblity to the mother country.

FRANCIS:

Don't we have a responsibility to our children...to build a peaceful world? Isn't that what we've always believed, Nell?

NELLIE:

I believe that freedom still has to be paid for. It's like a farm that has to be kept up. Another installment of the debt has fallen due. That's what I believe. There's a private in the Princess Pats who carries my picture in his cap, Francis. There are times when the doubter is intolerable!

FRANCIS looks from one to the other, then walks out.

Scene Three

FRANCIS is at her desk at the paper, writing an editorial.

FRANCIS:

When a coincidence of engagements brought Sir Robert Borden and Mrs. Nellie L. McClung to Winnipeg together recently, McClung made use of the opportunity to ask the Prime Minister to grant the federal franchise to all British and Canadian born women, excluding the foreign women.

In this, Mrs. McClung was speaking for herself alone, and not for the organized women of the suffrage provinces. I hope that the majority of the women who fought and won the suffrage fight, on the ground that democracy is right, still believe in democracy.

Personally, if I had a religious faith or a political conviction which wouldn't stand the test of a great crisis, and which had to be discarded whenever an emergency arose, I would rise up and take it out and bury it in a nice deep grave and pray that it might have no resurrection day!

For my part, I believe in democracy just as invincibly today as I did in the yesterday of my own political minority, and if a serious attempt is made to exclude these new women citizens from the franchise, my tongue and pen will do their little best by way of protest.

F.M.B.

FRANCIS opens her mail.

WOMAN:

Dear Miss Beynon:

You say that Mrs. McClung was speaking for herself alone, but I say her instincts as a patriot told her the right thing. My husband Jake and our three sons are in the war now and they're all of voting age. Yet their voices won't be heard. The foreign women have their husbands safe and sound by their sides and we all envy them. They may think differently and they may not, but how can we be sure? I think perhaps we should not take the chance.

Sincerely...Lonely at Home

Dear Miss Beynon:
I think that Lonely at Home should have five votes, not just one! One for herself and four for the manhood she has sent off to war! And I say, more power to Mrs. McClung's elbow! You say you believe in democracy. Well democracy means government by the people. In this crisis I say British people! Shall our men go and fight the Hun across the sea while their country is being turned over to a foreign power? A thousand times NO!

Fiercely...Wolfwillow

> *FRANCIS puts down the letters, gets up and puts on her coat.*

Scene Four

The train station. Sounds of the train sighing and hissing. FRANCIS is helping LILY with her suitcases. They are both agitated, upset.

LILY:

Vernon took the two big suitcases when he left last week. I've got my hat boxes. I guess that's everything. *looking lost* That's all, I guess.

FRANCIS: *handing her a book*
I've brought you a book. Carl Sandburg.

LILY:

Thank you.

FRANCIS:

Have you eaten? They probably won't serve lunch till one.

LILY:

I've just had breakfast. I couldn't eat another thing.

FRANCIS:

I made you some cookies to have with tea.

LILY:

Thank you.

FRANCIS:

Did you write Mother and give her your new address in New York?

LILY:

No. Could you do that, Fanny?

FRANCIS:
Oh, Lily!

LILY:
Fanny, please!

FRANCIS:
What should I tell her?

LILY:
Tell her Vernon's been offered a good job in New York and couldn't pass it up. Do you think she'd believe that? Tell her I'm going to be the new editor of *The New York Times*. Oh, I don't know what to tell her!

FRANCIS:
Why not tell her the truth? That Vernon walked onto the floor of the Legislature to shake hands with the only politician with enough courage to make an anti-conscription speech.

LILY:
Don't tell her that.

FRANCIS:
And for that he was fired! So you decided to go to a country where democracy still means something.

LILY:
Oh, I should have done it myself.

NELLIE arrives and looks from one to the other.

NELLIE:
Hello, Francis.   *to LILY*   Lily, I wanted to say goodbye.

LILY:
Oh, I'm glad you came.

They hug.

NELLIE:
Here's a book for the train.

LILY:

Kipling! Fanny brought me Sandburg. *She looks from one to the other.*

NELLIE:
Have you had anything to eat? It takes forever for them to serve lunch. Here's some biscuits.

LILY:

Fanny brought me some cookies! The two of you will have me rolling off the train in New York. *looking from one to the other* Well, here we are. The carefree sisters of the typewriter and interrogation mark. Any parting shots? *She grabs both of their hands.*

FRANCIS:
I still don't know the difference between baking soda and baking powder. I'm going to send the hard questions on to you in New York.

NELLIE:
I'll never forgive Vernon for taking you away.

LILY:

Vernon had no choice, Nell. No one will hire him here now. At least in New York, he can write about what he believes.

NELLIE:
You mean he can make a mockery of what our boys are fighting for!

FRANCIS:
That's not what he's doing!

LILY:

Please, please, let's not talk about Vernon. Let's talk about ourselves. Can we? I feel so helpless right now. It

used to be we'd talk about love and sisterhood...now
we only talk about death and destruction. Will you take
care of Fanny while I'm gone, Nell?

NELLIE:
Of course I will.

FRANCIS:
I'll be fine on my own.

NELLIE:
You're very hard on people, Francis. When the war is
over, we'll get the suffrage issue straightened out and
there'll be a vote for everyone. Believe me, just like
we've always dreamed. When the war is over.

CONDUCTOR: *offstage*
All aboard!

FRANCIS:
Have you got everything, Lily?

NELLIE:
I have to go. I've got two meetings before lunch. It
never ends. Write big long letters. Goodbye, Lily.

LILY and NELLIE hug. NELLIE exits.

LILY:
She was apologizing to you and you wouldn't accept it.
I understand how Nellie feels. She supports the war
because her son is fighting in it. She has no choice. But
that's no reason to turn your back on her, your best
friend, your teacher, just because she didn't meet your
high standards. How arrogant you are!

FRANCIS:
But she gave up her dream.

LILY:

No she didn't! She just lost sight of it for a while. It happens to all of us, and it will happen to you. You'll marry McNair and have children, and you won't be so eager to pick up a banner or lead a parade. You'll shift your zeal and compassion to those you love...and the dream won't seem so crystal clear any more!

FRANCIS:

If that's the price of love, I'm not sure I can pay it. I want to be free, Lily. I don't know what more to say than that.

LILY:

Fanny, you're never really free. You can frame a declaration of independence every day, but you won't be free. We're bound by our affections more than any legal contracts, or governments or causes. We're all trapped by something. The heart doesn't choose wisely, it just chooses.

Sound of the train whistle. Both sisters fight back tears.

FRANCIS:

Oh, don't leave. I don't know what I'll do without you.

LILY:

I've got to. It's time.

FRANCIS:

I love you, Lily.

LILY:

Fanny, you're a brick.

They hug. LILY leaves.

Scene Five

FRANCIS enters her office. McNAIR is there. She takes off her hat and coat.

FRANCIS:
> I've got four typewriters now—mine, Lily's and two of Vernon's—and none of them work very well. Have you ever been to New York, McNair?

McNAIR:
> I landed there when I first came over. I read a different paper every day for two weeks, and never found the same opinion twice. Don't worry, Francis. They'll find work.

FRANCIS:
> I guess so. McNair, do you think I'm...hard on people?

McNAIR:
> Very! You're like a terrier worrying a bone.

FRANCIS:
> Why do you think that is?

McNAIR:
> Because you've got a vision of the world that's clearer than most.

FRANCIS:
> Then why do I feel so frightened all the time... frightened that I'm wrong, or that I'm right, that I'm not doing enough, or that I'm doing too much...that I'll end up alone. When I was given a mind that questioned everything, why wasn't I given a spirit that feared nothing? I used to think that everything was possible, but I just don't know any more.

McNAIR:

> You're just tired, Francis, and you miss Lily. Why don't you open your mail? That will put the fight back into you.

> *FRANCIS opens her letters.*

WOMAN:

> Dear Miss Beynon:
> I say hurray for Borden and conscription. Let's round up those slackers who are hanging around the city poolrooms and get them into uniform. The time has come to send more than socks and tobacco to our heroes in the fighting line. What we need is Men Men and more Men!
>
> Western Sister

FRANCIS:

> Dear Western Sister: It is easy for us to be brave with other people's lives, but I don't believe in their hearts that the people of Canada want compulsory enlistment. Let's have a referendum to ask Canadians whether they want conscription!

WOMAN:

> Dear Miss Beynon:
> Referendum? Referendum now? For three years our boys have fought for us and our cause. Referendum now, while our enemy prepares destruction for our battered heroes? Surely not referendum but reinforcement! And quickly to our waiting sons!

> Dear Miss Beynon:
> What we are fighting here is a holy war against the very Prince of Darkness, and therefore every man owes it to God to support conscription. And if there is any man out there who says his conscience won't allow him to slay his fellow man, then he's laying down too strict a rule for his conscience.

FRANCIS:
> That is not God's plan! I believe that God is
> democracy, the only true democracy. He filled the
> world with human beings, no two of whom are alike
> and I'm sure he meant them to be left free to develop
> their differences and to report on life as they see it. War
> has never been in God's plan—the Lord of Peace—
> only that of man.

WOMAN:
> Dear Miss Know-It-All:
> "There shall be wars and rumours of war, but the end
> is not yet." Do not go taking the name of the Lord in
> vain and putting your half-cooked ideas on him. You
> used to be alright when you talked about votes for
> women, but you're a disgrace to the female race the
> way you go on about peace. Anyone who talks like that
> is a traitor and probably has foreign friends.

> *FRANCIS takes over the reading of the letter from the
> woman who has written it. She reads it aloud as
> McNAIR comes into the room.*

FRANCIS:
> "My husband told me to say that he's proud of his
> country and proud to fight for it, and if you don't keep
> your mouth shut, you might find someone will shut it
> for you."

McNAIR: *taking the letter from FRANCIS*
> This is a threat! Who wrote this?

FRANCIS:
> Would you sign a letter like this?

McNAIR:
> This has got to stop. You've gone too far!

FRANCIS:
> I've gone too far?

84

McNAIR:

When it gets to the point that people are sending you hate mail, like this, yes! People who write letters like this are unbalanced. You might get hurt, Francis.

FRANCIS:

It was you who told me that if I believe in something, I should have the courage to write about it.

McNAIR:

But this is different. The war is making people crazy. A man was nearly beaten to death at an anti-conscription rally last night. These are dangerous times. Where are you going?

FRANCIS has risen. She puts on her hat and coat.

FRANCIS:

To a meeting.

McNAIR:

What meeting?

FRANCIS:

A women's meeting, McNair, at the library. Nellie McClung is giving a talk. I'd like to hear what she has to say.

McNAIR:

I'll walk you there.

FRANCIS:

Thank you.

They exit together.

Scene Six

*A women's meeting. NELLIE is addressing the
audience.*

NELLIE:
> The Wartime Elections Act has just given us Dominion
> women the vote, and I think we should use it to vote
> for conscription. Yesterday, I received a letter from my
> son in France asking when we're going to send more
> troops. He says they're holding on as best they can, but
> they're getting weaker. Are we backing our boys or
> not? A thousand voices chatter reasons for delay, but
> across the seas comes one voice loud and clear. Who
> calls Canada? Our boys are calling us! Tonight is the
> beginning of the federal election campaign and the
> issue is conscription. Now is our chance to work for the
> candidates who are going to help our boys. We have no
> time to lose. The more women we can get out the
> better....

FRANCIS:
> Mrs. McClung, I have a question?

NELLIE:
> We don't have much time.

FRANCIS:
> I won't be long. How can our boys be fighting for
> freedom if we are not giving them the freedom to
> decide whether or not they'll give their lives?

NELLIE:
> That's not an easy question to answer. I've struggled
> with it in my heart. But sometimes, individual freedom
> has to be sacrificed for collective freedom. Peace can

only be achieved when we band together and let the enemy know that we will not budge.

FRANCIS:

I have another question.

NELLIE:

We have a lot of work to do.

FRANCIS:

How can peace be achieved, how can we get any nearer to peace, when a lot more people are being sacrificed?

NELLIE:

I think you're trying to be disruptive, Miss Beynon. Your views on the war are well known. I don't know whether there's any point in taking up more time.

FRANCIS:

Please, I'd just like to make one suggestion. *She goes up to the front.* Why don't we tell the politicians that we women, the mothers, wives and sisters of Canada, want to bring this war to a peaceful conclusion right now, before any more blood is shed!

NELLIE:

If there aren't any more questions, we should get down to forming committees. We have six candidates to start working for...

FRANCIS:

Can I talk for a minute please...just a minute! The real issue of this war is not conscription or the war over there. The real issue is being fought right here in halls like these. The real issue is whether militarism shall grow and prosper or whether it shall decline and fall. We, as women, in our first chance to use our franchise, are being asked to vote for war! To vote for sending more sons and husbands away to fight and be killed.

Let's use our vote to say NO to war! And let's not exclude our sisters because they speak another language—

WOMAN IN AUDIENCE:
Shut up. Just shut up! You don't know what you're talking about! You've got nothing to lose! Get out of here! GET OUT!

NELLIE:
Please, can we have order. Miss Beynon, I believe you have your answer. Now, let's get back to business.

FRANCIS leaves, anguished.

Scene Seven

The newspaper office. McNAIR is seated. FRANCIS storms into the office.

FRANCIS:

I just received a call from the censorship board. Those scoundrels told me not to write anything about the conscription bill which might ''arouse'' opposition!

McNAIR:

Sit down, Francis.

FRANCIS:

Since when have British citizens relinquished the right to discuss unmade legislation?

McNAIR:

Sit down, Francis.

FRANCIS:

Is this Canada or is this Prussia? Has everyone gone war mad?

McNAIR: *shouting*

Sit down, Francis!

FRANCIS finally sits.

I want to talk to you. I've been getting calls all week from readers. About you. One woman said she'd seen you handing out anti-war pamphlets at Portage and Main on two occasions, and that you were haranguing passers-by.

FRANCIS: *jumping up*
I was not haranguing them. I was trying to engage
them in conversation.

McNAIR:
The publisher called me a while ago. He's running for
parliament on the conscription issue. He wants me to...
he wants your resignation. I told him I would talk to
you.

FRANCIS: *in disbelief*
He wants me to resign from my job?

McNAIR:
Yes.

FRANCIS:
No! I won't! He can't get away with something like
that! We can get my readers to back me!

McNAIR:
Francis, your readers haven't been very supportive
lately.   *He slams the letters down on the desk.*
Haven't you noticed?

FRANCIS:
What about you?

McNAIR:
Don't you ever get tired of rowing upsteam?

FRANCIS:
McNair, what about you? The paper has a role to play
in presenting all sides of the war issue. We've got to get
people thinking! Really thinking! Really questioning!

McNAIR:
The issue has already been discussed to death. Borden
has granted the Empire women the vote and they're
going to use it to ram conscription down our throats!

FRANCIS:
> No! No!

McNAIR:
> Yes! And there's nothing you can do about it. Or
> should do about it!

FRANCIS:
> So you simply suspend freedom of the press...freedom
> to express opinions?

McNAIR:
> Nobody gives a damn about your opinions, or my
> opinions either! We've just got to win the war and then
> you can hold any damned opinion you like. Just
> swallow hard and hold on.

FRANCIS:
> Do you want me to resign?

McNAIR:
> Yes. No. I don't have any choice.

> *FRANCIS turns to leave.*

> Francis, wait. Look at me. Will you look at me.
> *FRANCIS turns.* You've got lines on your face now
> that don't go away when you stop smiling. I can see a
> hint of grey in your hair along the temples. You're not
> a young girl any more. Francis, I love you. I want to
> marry you. I want to take care of you. I want you to
> stop worrying about what you can't change. Let me
> take care of you now. Don't say anything. Let me talk.
> I've saved enough money to buy a house. Leave the
> paper. You won't have to put up with any more
> abusive letters, you won't have to turn yourself inside
> out with issues. I know how it tortures you. Just let it
> all go!

FRANCIS:
> McNair, I love my work.

McNAIR:

I know you do, Francis, but I'm asking you to marry me! You can forget about everything else.

FRANCIS shivers, moves away.

FRANCIS:

It's cold in here suddenly.   *slowly, with difficulty*
You said to me once that I was like a bird struggling to get free though it loved the warmth of your hand. I love you, McNair. I love your warmth. But I....   *Her voice breaks.*   can't...do what you want. It would be too much like a closed hand. And I'd always be straining to get free. Do you understand?

> *McNAIR searches her face, almost speaks, then thinks better of it. Instead, he comes over to FRANCIS, puts his arms around her, holds her for a moment, then leaves.*

> *FRANCIS is left standing alone. A wave of emotion flows over her as she realizes the extent of her aloneness now. A wail comes from deep inside her. She drops her head, remains silent for a long while, then slowly walks over to her desk and begins to collect up her belongings. As she begins to formulate her last editorial, we see her resolve and vision and brightness returning to her.*

FRANCIS:

Every once in a while, one comes to a parting of the ways. I have come to that today. It is with deep feelings of regret that I am severing my connection with *The Rural Review.* I had hoped through this page, that we women of the prairies could help advance the cause of women, and I believe that in some small ways, we have done that. It would have been a much bigger thing if we could have claimed to have erased tyranny and war and intolerance. I now think that that is a work to be measured in generations. But someday, when we who are here now are dead and gone, and the little acorns that were planted on our graves have grown into flourishing trees and fallen into decay, it will come to be recognized that there is no crime in being different, in doing one's own thinking. It may even be that in that dim and shadowy future, the world will have sense enough to value peace, and we will be able to live free of the fear of war. This, in the end, is the only thing that really matters. By the time this reaches print, I will have left for the Mecca of all writers on this continent, the city of New York. There, I will continue to work towards that future. One can only follow "The Gleam" as one sees it, and hope that it does not prove to be a will-o-the-wisp.

And that is all.

THE END